My Deepest Me

A 30-Day Retreat to Nourish Your Inner Life

Janice Lynne Lundy

Do you know what you are?

You are a manuscript of a divine letter.

You are a mirror reflecting a noble face.

This universe is not outside of you.

Look inside yourself;

everything that you want,

you are already that.

Jelaluddin Rumi

(Translated by Shahram Shiva)

Apocryphile Press
PO Box 255
Hannacroix, NY 12087
www.apocryphilepress.com

Please join our mailing list at www.apocryphilepress.com/free
We'll keep you up to date on all our new releases,
and we'll also send you a FREE BOOK. Visit us today!

Contents

Introduction

Historians report that she rushed into the streets shouting, "My deepest me is God!" It was 15th century Italy and unthinkable for a woman of her station in life to profess herself in such a way. Imagine the reactions of her family and friends! Catherine of Genoa was undoubtedly a spirit-filled woman willing to risk the good opinions of others to live in the only way she knew how—intimately connected to and passionate about the Divine.

How many of us would be willing to do what she did? How many of us even know who our "deepest me" is? I have spent most of my adult life pondering this. If we are in tune with our inner life to any degree, we know that there is someone deep within us who is well worth knowing, a version of ourselves that is not encumbered or hindered by the world. There is also a Source, a life-giving fount some of us might call "God." It is the journey of our lifetime to get to know both entities, and, ultimately, to decipher the relationship between the two. *My Deepest Me* is one way for you to begin that journey, or broaden it, if you have already embarked.

As a spiritual director and companion, I know the value of setting aside a designated amount of time to focus on our inner life. The world is a clamorous place, and we are constantly distracted from attending to our well-being—body, mind, heart, and soul. There is so much to pull us away from any real knowing of inner peace, unconditional love, or boundless joy. There is so much to distance us from the voice of the Sacred that speaks to us in softer tones to guide us along the way. "Time in," retreat time, is vital for our spiritual health.

Life's pace and responsibilities being what they are, many of us are unable to take dedicated retreat time. The book that you hold in your hands can serve as a guided retreat, done privately, in the ease of your own home. Or taken with you when you are fortunate enough one day to go on retreat. Used day-by-day, it can serve as a wise guide, inviting you to earnest inquiry about who you are in the truest sense, especially who you are in relationship to the One.

When Catherine of Genoa proclaimed her deepest me as God, she had come to a unique understanding through mystical experience that her inner peace, her love, her joy *was* her Source—and that this Source lived within her. It was not outside of her somewhere, a distant unfathomable entity, but breathing through her *as her.* This is a bold concept, and one characteristic of mystics from the beginning of time who had firsthand knowledge of an indwelling Spirit.

Today, most of us are not mystics like Catherine. We are practical folks, and most of the time all we really want from life is to feel less stressed, not so overwhelmed, or worried. We also desire to be peace-filled, loving and kind. Certainly, we want to feel the presence of the Divine within us but, for all practical purposes, the way we may experience God in the modern age *is* as peace or love. Knowing this, we could reframe for ourselves what Catherine also knew to be true: "My deepest me is love," or "My deepest me is peace." The longing to make manifest the "virtues of the spirit" in our own lives is the first sign of a desire to live as our deepest selves.

The month-long journey you will take with this book will expose you to new understandings of the virtues of the spirit. Each of the 30 days in *My Deepest Me* offers a gentle teaching that has the potential to shift your perspective about who you are as a sacred being, as well as who or what the Divine is to you. You will be encouraged to try out new contemplative practices that can take you deeper yet. Space is provided in the book for daily reflection—to listen and write about how the Spirit is moving in you.

On your guided retreat, you will also be invited to mine such inner treasures as:

> Identifying what pulls you away from sacred connection
> How to create daily "Soul Time"
> How to view everything that happens to you as "spiritual"
> Creating a new relationship with your breath as a holy encounter
> How to transform difficult thoughts and feelings into virtues of the spirit
> Growing self-compassion for the purpose of spiritual healing
> Experiencing Divine Presence in new and unforeseen ways

At the end of one month, you will have a much stronger sense of "your deepest you" and how that emboldened version is calling you to live in the world more publicly, and in service of others. We may not all shout our newfound faith to the world as Catherine did, but we can rest in the knowledge that we have responded well to a holy call to live a more authentic life. Hopefully, we will have come to know the Divine within us in a new, life-affirming way. Joan Chittister, OSB, might describe what we now know as truth this way: "The God within us, our 'deepest,' is exactly what connects us to the rest of life—to other people, to nature, to wholeness of spirit."

My highest hope is that *My Deepest Me* will serve as a trustworthy companion for your inner journey and that you will feel my love and support all along the way. Please know that I continue to strengthen my own understanding of my deepest me. I write this book not because I have arrived at any pinnacle of peace or faithfulness, but because I am committed to augmenting what I know by sharing it with others for our common good.

We are divinely made and lovingly crafted. Let us dedicate ourselves to a more profound knowing and sharing of this sacred truth.

How to Use This Book

On the spiritual path, it is good and wise to have a guide to point the way, or, at the very least, a map that illumines the path for us. Without a trusty escort, we may wander in the desert of delusion or get stuck in the brambles of ego. This "30-Day Retreat" book is designed to serve as a trusty companion and way-shower for your inner journey.

Without focus and steadfast effort, our spiritual life can be vague and ineffectual. Dedicating one entire month to strengthening a particular aspect of it is not only enriching, but life altering, too.

Beginning with Day 1, each entry in the book will take you into a deeper understanding of one important spiritual truth about your deepest you, then, invite you to implement it by practicing it.

The "Going Deeper" segment of each entry will serve as fodder for inner growth. There are reflection questions and/or a spiritual practice to try on for size.

Take time each day to reflect upon your experience in the "Inner Listening" section. Here, you will get to know yourself just as you are. Reflective writing can reveal further insights. Contemplating in this way also sheds light on what you are doing right, which provides impetus for your ongoing journey. There are additional pages of this sort with writing prompts and inspirational quotes at the end of the book.

The "Knowing" statement that accompanies each daily entry summarizes the truth you are coming to know and can serve as a reminder of what to stay focused on as the days unfold.

As you conclude the daily portion of this book, you will be invited to reflect upon and integrate the totality of your experience in "The Afterwards" section.

Give yourself plenty of permission as you journey through this month. If you need longer than one day for a particular entry, take the time to do that. Trust that the Spirit is guiding you at the pace you need. If you skip a day or fall behind, begin again. The beauty of any given day is that we *can* start over; every day offers a new opportunity to deepen our awareness of self and Spirit.

If you are currently in a formal relationship with a spiritual director or companion, share this guided retreat experience with them. Ongoing support for your journey is vital and your companion would want to know what is stirring in you.

If you are a spiritual director, mentor, or guide yourself, this book can serve as an excellent resource and practice ground for those whom you companion. The truths shared within are inter-spiritual in nature, drawn from the "perennial tradition," as Fr. Richard Rohr describes it. Seekers of all traditions can find sustenance within these pages. *My Deepest Me* is useful for spiritual direction sessions because it showcases many of the mindsets and practices that we hope to cultivate for a Spirit-centered life. It will enhance the good work you are doing with others and provide a common framework for inner growth. And, as a spiritual companion, you may find it to be a useful tool for transparency and deepening for yourself, too!

Blessings of deep peace to you, faithful traveler. May you know wholeness and the joy of holy newness. May Grace surround you and enfold you every day of your life.

All Love,
Jan Lundy

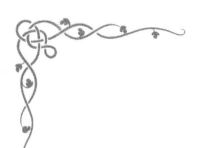

DAY 1
Your Heart's Longing

There comes a time when we know we need to live in a new way. Whatever it is we're doing isn't working very well. We may feel unhappy with our life as it is. Perhaps we feel lost, confused, or ready for a significant change. We may be facing a health challenge, struggling with a relationship, or feeing dissatisfied with our work. In the physical sense, the heart appears to be longing for more, or at least for things to be different than they are.

On a higher level, the longing of your heart may be much more than a human hunger for a better life. It may be that the Divine One is calling you "home," inviting you into greater self-awareness and communion. You have been placed on this earth to be a purveyor of peace, love, and joy, generosity, hope, and kindness. If you are not being that, nor experiencing these "virtues of the spirit" within yourself on a regular basis, then something may be amiss. Your dissatisfaction may be nothing less than a sacred invitation to live in a very different way.

You can begin to forge a new, soul-nourishing relationship with the Sacred—beginning today.

Going Deeper

1. What does your heart long for these days? Meaningful and well-paid work? Healing from health woes? Fewer relationship challenges? What wearies your body, preoccupies your mind, and troubles your heart?

2. On the spiritual path, honesty is vital. We can fool ourselves, but not the Divine Mind. Be transparent as you answer and reflect upon this question: What do you truly ache for, desire more than anything else, when it comes to your *inner* life?

3. When you acknowledge these longings, do you have a sense of what the Sacred is inviting you to right now?

Inner Listening

_____

_____

_____

_____

_____

_____

_____

_____

_____

_____

_____

Knowing

Dissatisfaction with my "outer life" may be a symptom of a deeper malaise, indicating where I am out of alignment with my true calling, where I need to heal and grow.

NOTE: Throughout this book, I will use the terms the "Sacred" or "Divine" to denote our cross-cultural/inter-spiritual understanding of ultimate reality, God, Presence, the All, Spirit, Brahman, Essence, etc. This encompasses, in my view, any term we might use to describe our knowing of transcendent experience of life and of true Self. We each must find our unique way of expressing this. As you read, feel free to substitute the words and names by which you know the Holy.

DAY 2
Stretching Toward the One

We've all heard a great deal in recent years about "the power of intention" with numerous books written on the subject. An intention is a consolidated hope around a specific desire or goal. It is what you deeply desire for yourself, like a meaningful inner life and a vibrant relationship with the Sacred. An intention is made manifest when you focus, commit, and are willing to put some muscle behind your words. A strongly-held intention allows you to release and transform what is not working in your life—to embrace that which will return you to right relationship with the Holy. It also heals us and allows us to reclaim our wholeness.

The Middle English origin of the word *intention* implies *stretching* or *purpose*. When we clarify our intention, we begin to stretch toward that which brings real results. Our effort holds the highest purpose because we are willing to make a commitment, to sign a sacred contract with our deepest self to live in the most virtue-laden way possible. Then we dig in and make the effort. We stretch ourselves, and, in the stretching, we reach out toward the One who awaits our return.

Going Deeper

1. Identify the primary intention that you are willing to hold in your heart and work toward for the next 30 days. Perhaps it is to feel sacred presence more often. Or to embody a virtue of the spirit that has eluded you like inner peace, gratitude, or unconditional love. Perhaps it is to re-dedicate yourself to a spiritual practice that you've let slide. Ask for guidance to be shown which area of your inner life needs your time and attention.

2. Once you have identified your intention, infuse it with heart energy, making it a solemn promise, not unlike the vows taken by people in holy orders. Write a statement of intention, beginning with the words, "I will ..."

3. In the silence of your heart-mind, visualize yourself reaching out toward Source and being lovingly met, supported, and guided to make this intention your reality.

Inner Listening

_____

_____

_____

_____

_____

_____

_____

_____

_____

_____

_____

_____

_____

_____

_____

_____

_____

_____

Knowing

Personal change begins with intention. Spiritual transformation occurs when I bring my whole self to the process and trust that I will be met halfway.

DAY 3
Naming the "Nameless"

How do you understand the Divine? By what name do you know the Unknowable?

As you deepen your relationship with yourself and the Sacred, it is good and wise to spend some time clarifying this. You may have been raised in a certain religious tradition—or none. The spiritual understanding of your childhood may not be relevant anymore or, being without a root tradition, you may be searching for one that is relevant for you today. In fact, this is one of the most important milestones on the spiritual path: to develop a mature understanding of the Divine and our unique relationship to it.

We explore "naming" so our relationship with the Divine is personally meaningful, so it has importance and relevance for who we are today. In her book, *Fragments of Your Ancient Name*, Joyce Rupp, OSM, presents 365 "glimpses of the Divine," or names of "God" that have been used worldwide since recorded time. Imagine, 365 names! We are constantly evolving beings and our relationship with Source must evolve too, especially, if it is to serve us well in a complex, demanding world … and for us to be purveyors of its love and joy for the healing of humanity.

Going Deeper

1. Moslems proclaim 100 names of Allah in their prayers. Jews, on the other hand, are forbidden from saying the name of G_D and may refer to it as *hashem*, "the name."

   What is your name for the "God of your understanding"? The All, Universe, Love, Truth, the Almighty, Beingness, Mother, Beloved, Universal Soul, Friend, Abba, Basic Goodness, Allah, and Sophia are some examples. Our names for the Holy are numerous, yet if we are to enter into an intimate relationship with "He," "She," or "It," is good to have vocabulary that fosters meaningful connection and intimacy.

2. What does the name you've identified mean to you? What message does it convey to your heart?

3. Explore other names— perhaps try on multiple names for size—names that will allow you to connect with an all-inclusive, expansive understanding of the Divine.

Inner Listening

_____

_____

_____

_____

_____

_____

_____

_____

_____

_____

_____

_____

_____

_____

_____

_____

_____

Knowing

The boundaries I put around my understanding of God can keep me small, stuck, and disconnected from the boundless nature of the divine mind and my ever-evolving soul.

DAY 4
Acknowledging Interference

On the spiritual path, it's wise to say "what is," to tell the truth about our human experience. It's helpful to transparently identify what takes us away from attending to our inner life. Many of us today find ourselves wearing the badge of honor that proclaims, "I'm so busy!" As the pace of our lives accelerates ("So many things to do, so many responsibilities."), we are invited to choose, again and again, that which feels imminent, more important, over what might be conducive to spiritual connection. In other words, we have plenty of excuses for not having time to connect with the Sacred.

It's true, we are busy! Such is the nature of life today. But when we neglect that which sustains us and brings us peace, we do not honor the importance of our inner life. Like bees in a hive, we work so hard at making honey that we've forgotten the joy of tasting, touching, and savoring the joys of sacred connection. We struggle with agitated bodies, turbulent minds, and closed hearts because we've ignored the healing power and necessity of being still, being prayerful, and resting into Love. Cultivating the virtues of the spirit takes time but doing so will provide much needed relief from the chaos and cacophony of life.

Going Deeper

1. With transparency, acknowledge what interferes with your inner life. What aspects of your life take you away from Spirit rather than toward it?

2. When you do have time in your day to engage in sacred connection (spiritual practice), what excuses do you have? What speaks to you as being more important? Acknowledge these excuses. Write them upon the page here, so when you hear them, you can make a new, wise choice.

3. Awareness, they say is half the battle. When you find yourself caught up in excuse-making, stop, listen, and acknowledge this interference. Take a few conscious breaths

and make a new choice. Choose Spirit over chores—even for as little as five minutes a day. Remember that you are a human being, not a human doing.

Inner Listening

_____

_____

_____

_____

_____

_____

_____

_____

_____

_____

_____

_____

_____

_____

_____

_____

_____

_____

_____

_____

Knowing

It is good to be active, productive, and useful, but when busyness overshadows the beauty and benefit of spiritual connection, I diminish my relationship with the Sacred.

DAY 5
Remembering Who You Really Are

Do you believe that you are a spiritual being, a sacred and holy person? Or do you believe that you are a tragically flawed human who must strive for acceptance, for perfection? Or perhaps do you hold a viewpoint somewhere in between?

No matter your answer, rest assured it is the perfect one for you—for now. It affirms who you think you are in this moment and, in the eyes of the Divine One, you are perfect just the way you are. Even if you perceive yourself to be lost or disconnected, it is still the right place to be—for now. If you are committed to connecting more deeply with your sacred self, and are willing to remain open to new possibilities, you will deepen in self-awareness, and your true self will be revealed.

Your true self, your deepest self, is comprised of the qualities you attribute to Spirit itself—peacefulness, loving-kindness, generosity, and more. These qualities make up your essence—the truth of who you really are. Your life task is to uncover this sacred essence, which, until now, may have been camouflaged, masked, by the ego or false self. You do not need to strive to access your essence. Simply drop down within yourself and spend more time with it. You will come to know it well.

Going Deeper

1. How do you feel about yourself as a sacred being, a divinely-sourced human being? Does this concept resonate with you? Why or why not?

2. Do you see yourself through lenses of love and compassion as the Divine might see you? A beautiful being who is in the process of remembering her/his true nature?

3. Are you in touch with your essence on a regular basis? With the peace, love, and generosity that naturally reside in you?

Inner Listening

_____

_____

_____

_____

_____

_____

_____

_____

_____

_____

_____

_____

_____

_____

_____

_____

_____

Knowing

Life is a pilgrimage of rediscovering my true self. It is a powerful voyage of inner communion and God connection, reclaiming who I really am in the mind and heart of God.

DAY 6
The Effortless Practice

When we think of spiritual practices, we may consider them time-consuming or difficult. If this is our mindset, we will tend to avoid them or make excuses to not do them. There is one practice, however, that is effortless, one that can plug us into the Divine in a nanosecond—the sacred breath.

This breath is not your everyday, stress-releasing breath, not yoga breath, or Lamaze breath. It is a holy breath, one that is sourced in the creation stories of many religious traditions. In Creek (American Indian) mythology, there was a being who lived on a hill, Esaugeteh Emisee, "the master of breath," and he created humanity. The Creator in the Hebrew/Christian tradition breathed man into existence. The breath has long been associated with the One who gives life. And that it does. With every breath we take, we are mysteriously enlivened, gently carried into the next precious moment of our lives.

Our breath is often an under-appreciated gift. The wise ones of the past have told us for eons that the first sign of divine presence is a feeling of deep inner peace. Connecting with your breath in a sacred manner is the effortless practice that can take you there.

Going Deeper

1. Reframe your breath to represent "portable peace," an on-the-go spiritual practice. Set the intention to take peaceful pauses throughout the day to plug back into your inner calm and the Sacred. (The trick, of course, is remembering to do it!)

2. When breathing, take slow measured inhales and exhales. Don't focus on the breath per se, but on *being breathed*—feeling the breath move effortlessly through you. Breath by gentle breath, you are being restored and welcomed "home" by Source. Say silently to yourself, "I am being breathed." How does this feel?

3. You may wish to take this practice one step further, breathing slowly and evenly, matching your inhales and exhales with the words, "God is breathing me." Feel the blessing of this and record in your journal how it feels to breathe this way.

Inner Listening

_____

_____

_____

_____

_____

_____

_____

_____

_____

_____

_____

_____

_____

_____

_____

_____

_____

Knowing

Connection with Spirit is as close as my breath, is my breath, when I bring attention to the holiness of everyday breathing.

DAY 7
Finding Your Ideal Practice

We have all witnessed others engaged in meaningful spiritual practices. Bearded men garbed in black, bobbing rhythmically at the Wailing Wall in Jerusalem. White-robed swamis chanting "Hare Krishna." Sufi Dervishes whirling. African drummers drumming. All these and more fill our imaginations, hopeful that we, too, might find practices that enliven our spirit.

Spiritual practices, simply put, are those activities that connect us more deeply with the virtues of the spirit, with the Divine itself, by whatever name we call it. They are practices that provide us with a unique opportunity to experience sacred time and space; to remove ourselves from the distractions and noise of a too busy world and remember our spiritual connection. Spiritual practices, properly cultivated, enable us to access inner calm, joy, and gratitude for life.

The variety of spiritual practices available to us is boundless. There are quiet practices: various forms of prayer, meditation, silence, or sacred reading; active practices: singing, chanting, dancing, worship, or creative expression; and physical practices: yoga, bowing, tai chi, gardening, or mindful walking. Spiritual practices can be done alone or with others; in one's home, in nature, in a church, temple or mosque. At all times of day or night. Have you identified yours?

Going Deeper

1. Have you given yourself complete permission to explore the wide variety of practices available to you? Or are you stuck in practices from childhood that may have lost their meaning? Is there anything that prevents you from exploring, from expanding? Peer pressure, organizational dictates, or the "good opinion" of others?

2. When you do engage in a particular practice, how does it make you feel? What virtues of the spirit rise? How do you experience the Sacred?

3. If your current practice is not bringing you benefit, consider mixing it up a bit. Try something new. Dare to bring yourself to new spiritual terrain, even if it feels slightly uncomfortable. Listen to what your body-mind says and honor its wisdom.

Inner Listening

_____

_____

_____

_____

_____

_____

_____

_____

_____

_____

_____

_____

_____

_____

_____

Knowing

If my heart is open and pure, if my intention is clear, God will meet me wherever I am: the pew, the mat, the woods. All are of the One.

DAY 8
Making a Commitment

With dedication, we will locate the "right" practices for us. By staying faithful to them, we will begin to experience their deeper benefits. The key is dailyness. It takes time for spiritual practices to work their magic upon us—to root us more deeply in the qualities of the spirit. Psychologists tell us it takes 21 days to create any new habit, 90 days for that habit to stick. Spiritual practices are no exception. It may take a year or more for them to become an invaluable part of our lifestyle.

In time, the lines of distinction between ourselves and our practice will begin to blur. We actually *become* the practice. Its benefits—inner calm and openheartedness—meld into us. One day we may awaken to realize that we not only *feel* more loving, we have *become* more loving; that we do not just *feel* more peaceful, but that we have become a peaceful presence in the world. Our friends and family confirm this. They tell us we are different; that we have changed for the better.

But first you must commit to the practice. To honor your deepest self, as well as your relationship to the Divine, you must make your chosen spiritual practice a priority. No matter what is happening in your life you can certainly find some time each day to engage the Sacred. Right?

Going Deeper

1. To which spiritual practice are you willing to commit for this 30-day journey? Begin with as little as five minutes a day so the practice doesn't feel burdensome and to strengthen your spiritual muscles. In time, you may want to extend your practice—15-30 minutes, even an hour—if it feels satisfying and connective.

2. Make a commitment and stick to it. How long will your practice be? What time of day will you do it? How many days a week will you do it?

3. Consider customizing your daily practice by combining practices into a meaningful routine. Morning prayer with meditation. Gentle yoga and a walk in nature. Devotional reading and journaling. This is *your* practice, and there is no one way to create it. Make your practice your own. A practice that is meaningful and enjoyable will be easier to maintain. Make it your special offering to the Divine.

Inner Listening

_____

_____

_____

_____

_____

_____

_____

_____

_____

_____

_____

_____

_____

_____

_____

Knowing

Sustained spiritual practice is a powerful path to awakening. If I give myself fully to the practice, the Holy will meet me where I am. Healing will happen.

DAY 9
Beyond Perfection

Vigilance, faithfulness, to one's practice is important on the spiritual path. As Joan Gattuso reminds us, "Without spiritual discipline we are never going to wake up or advance on our journey through this life." It's true, if we are not alert, our spiritual practice can become shoddy and prone to excuses. Spiritual laziness is a real danger. It is good to be watchful for these tendencies.

On the other hand, we can also place too much pressure on ourselves to get our practice exactly right. Unconsciously we may strive to become the perfect pray-er, meditator, devotee, or disciple. Our practice can become a source of pressure and angst because we have burdened it and ourselves with unhealthy "shoulds" and expectations. We live in a culture that focuses on human perfection, and sometimes, mistakenly, we link the quality and frequency of our practice to some sort of divine reward system.

Wisdom resides in walking a middle path. We keep our eyes on the goal of practice (self-realization, God-realization), yet at the same time, we treat ourselves kindly and gently. Spiritual progress is not about achievement but about accessing more gentle places within us. Quiet places where we can hear our own compassionate voice saying, "Rest"; where we hear a divine voice whisper, "Welcome home." "Progress not perfection," is a wise mantra to keep.

Going Deeper

1. Are you harboring any unhealthy "shoulds" about your spiritual practice? If so, what are they?

2. Be aware of your self-talk when you think about your spiritual practice. Do you have high expectations for yourself? Do you tend to rate the quality of your experience when your "time in" is over?

3. Practice setting aside any critical voices you may hear when you engage your practice. Cultivate a self-compassionate voice instead, one that might say, "You are doing fine." "I am glad you are here." "Let go and let God." "Just be."

Inner Listening

_____

_____

_____

_____

_____

_____

_____

_____

_____

_____

_____

_____

_____

_____

_____

_____

_____

Knowing

My spiritual practice can be a resting place where I meet the Divine as I am—without expectations, pressures or "shoulds." I believe that each time I bring myself to the practice I am making inner progress.

DAY 10
Everything Is Spiritual

We tend to compartmentalize our lives into *spiritual* and *non-spiritual*. We may think that our inner life is separate from, even superior to, our daily life. In truth, it's all the same thing. Everything is spiritual. *Everything.*

Every human encounter invites us to more: to look at how well we are embodying the spiritual values we claim to hold dear, how well we are walking our spiritual talk— genuinely *being* the spiritual persons we claim ourselves to be. In fact, it is within the context of human relationship that we'll learn the most about ourselves.

Living in the "real" world—going to work or school, being partnered, having kids, living in a neighborhood—*is* how we come to know ourselves as divinely-sourced, but completely human beings. We intend to love fully yet close our hearts in anger. We preach generosity but hold tight to our wallets when we spot a homeless person on the street.

The truth is, we are perfectly imperfect and, because we are, life offers us one opportunity after another to grow. As mysterious as it might sound, every human being, every experience, can be a teacher to us.

Going Deeper

1. Do you tend to see your inner life as separate from your daily life of duties and human interaction? Do you see your inner life as sacred and your "regular" life as secular, even profane?

2. What is the one area of your life that is causing you the most difficulty? Consider that, right now, this arena holds your greatest spiritual invitation. It is where the Spirit is nudging you to grow.

3. Acknowledging this difficulty as an invitation, what is Spirit nudging you toward? To be more loving or kind? Generous or forgiving? Courageous or faithful? Name the virtue of the spirit that is beckoning you to integration, so that your outer life reflects your inner life.

Inner Listening

_____

_____

_____

_____

_____

_____

_____

_____

_____

_____

_____

_____

_____

_____

_____

_____

_____

Knowing

Everything I experience in life is sacred because everything that happens to me is laden with holy purpose: to help me take a deeper look at how I am living in the world.

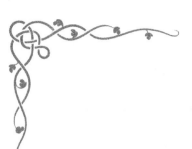

DAY 11
A Vow of Transparency

The key to living a rich-in-Spirit life lies in our ability to be "transparent." This means we are so passionate about our inner journey that we are willing to look at ourselves openly and honestly. We acknowledge our history, our patterns, and the stories we continue to tell ourselves.

Being transparent means you can no longer hide from anything—especially from yourself. It is wise to do so in a spirit of curiosity and wonder, with joy and gratitude, because you have the blessed opportunity to get to know yourself in a healthy, new way. If you desire healing and wholeness, truth-telling is important.

Transparency also means that there is no more hiding from Source either, because, more than anything, we desire a deep and meaningful, authentic relationship with the One.

We do this journey with a warm and loving heart. We are gentle with ourselves. We go slowly and treat ourselves kindly. We let go of notions of perfection, of getting it right, or being the most spiritual person on the block. We do what we can when we can and pat ourselves on the back all along the way.

Going Deeper

1. At this juncture of your inner journey, are you willing to take a vow of transparency? Are you willing to tell the truth about yourself and your life? About your relationship with the Divine?

2. What may prevent you from being open and honest with yourself, with the Divine, about what needs healing attention?

3. When you listen to your heart, what does it have to say to you about how you are living right now?

Inner Listening

_____

_____

_____

_____

_____

_____

_____

_____

_____

_____

_____

_____

_____

_____

_____

_____

Knowing

Being open and honest with myself, with the God of my understanding, is the first step in creating the life I am meant to live—one of wholeness and joy.

DAY 12
Soul Time

Our lives have become busy and complex. For some of us, there seems to be very little "down time" anymore. We move from activity to activity with minimal awareness of our soul's needs. It is vital that we take "Soul Time," "time in," to be alone with our sacred self and Spirit; to regain our footing, to access inner calm and the clarity that naturally arises when we do. Ensconced in perpetual busyness, we may neglect our soul and become disconnected from its guiding voice.

"Soul Time" is a regularly scheduled time each day to sit with your soul and commune with it—breathe with it, feel its presence—to feel it as *you*. Truly, we cannot hope to connect with our soul—much less listen to what it has to say—without sitting still and entering into quiet.

If we are in need of Soul Time, it's good to begin with just five minutes so that our time-in feels enjoyable, rather than burdensome, or like a spiritual "should." We engage this new practice in a manageable way; slowly, taking baby steps, because a new habit gently forged has staying power. Within days, we will begin to feel refreshed and nourished.

Going Deeper

1. To create your Soul Time, first look at the "schedule" of your day and find one 5-minute time slot you can spare. Five minutes, that's all! Choose the very best, easiest time of day for you so Soul Time does not feel like an imposition. Write "Soul Time" into your day planner. Prioritize this sacred time. Make it happen.

2. Two optimal periods for Soul Time are first thing in the morning when you wake up or before you go to bed at night. These are times when the mind tends to be less busy. We have just come out of or are entering sleep and the body/mind is more at ease.

3. Let go of any agenda for Soul Time except to just *be with* your experience as it unfolds. Just *BE* with yourself, your soul, in a sacred way. *Breathing and being. Breathing and being.* Rest, let go, be present to your sacred self in this very moment.

Inner Listening

_____

_____

_____

_____

_____

_____

_____

_____

_____

_____

_____

_____

_____

_____

_____

_____

Knowing

Even for as little as five minutes a day, I can begin to forge a new relationship with myself as a sacred being. My soul needs time and space to be heard. I will get to know myself on a soul level by resting with it in silence.

DAY 13
Getting Beneath Your Thoughts

What are your predominant thoughts? Perhaps you experience obsessive thinking or worrying, planning mind, judging mind, doubting mind, complaining mind, brooding mind, or comparing mind. Thought patterns like these can derail us from living as our best self. Thoughts like these can also drown out the voice of Spirit, that guiding presence that is always accessible—if we have the ears to listen and the heart to receive it.

You are not a "bad" person, or a less-than-spiritual one, because you have thoughts like these. Everyone does! In truth, your thoughts are not you. They come. They go. They change like the wind. One moment you may be thinking about pizza, the next about an argument you had with a neighbor. Thoughts are like clouds, constantly changing, and it is up to us to decide how much of our attention we wish to give them. Beneath all the thinking and ruminating, there is someone well worth knowing—you, *the real you, your deepest you*—which is sourced in the Spirit.

It is wise to create a more empowered relationship with your thoughts. It is good to engage with them discerningly. It is wise *and* good to determine if your thoughts are leading you toward greater peace, love, or joy—or if they are taking you into stress, anger, or despair.

Going Deeper

1. What kinds of thoughts do you experience on a regular basis that might keep you "off the path," disconnected from your spirit and the Divine? Worry? Self-Doubt? Fear? Rest assured; these thoughts are not you. They are just something you are experiencing.

2. Right now, take a few gentle breaths. Allow any disturbing thoughts that may be present to fall away. Remove your awareness from them and focus on your breath.

3. When you find yourself quieting, notice who is left beneath all those thoughts. You are—the essence of you! This is the "being" with whom you wish to stay connected—your calm, clear, wise self.

Inner Listening

_____

_____

_____

_____

_____

_____

_____

_____

_____

_____

_____

_____

_____

_____

_____

_____

_____

Knowing

I am an innately calm, clear, wise person at heart. Thoughts are simply thoughts. They are not me—not the deepest me. Inner peace is me. Love is me. Joy is me. This is my birthright and my destiny.

DAY 14
True Compassion

Our faith traditions tell us we are supposed to be patient, kind, and generous, but sometimes that's just plain hard to do. Life is challenging. People are too. Therefore it is important to learn to treat ourselves kindly—to treat ourselves as lovingly and tenderly as we would a dear friend or a precious child. Instead of being disappointed in ourselves for missing the mark or failing at embodying the spiritual virtues to which we aspire, we can choose another course of action: self-compassion.

In every spiritual tradition, compassion is highly valued. Compassion for ourselves, however, has often been aligned with self-absorption or selfishness. And we are not taught, nor encouraged, how to be self-compassionate.

In truth, self-compassion is one of the most powerful spiritual virtues we can adopt to walk peaceably in the world. First, we must learn to walk peaceably with ourselves. Then we can learn to walk this way with others. We cannot exhibit true compassion for others if we have not cultivated it for ourselves.

Going Deeper

1. Self-assess and reflect: How skilled are you at self-compassion? Do you talk nicely to yourself or are you self-critical? Do you make kind choices for yourself, or do you tend to push yourself? Do you have high expectations of yourself and find fault with yourself if you don't meet them?

2. Reflect on this teaching about self-compassion attributed to the Buddha: "You can search throughout the entire universe for someone who is more deserving of your love and affection than you are yourself, and that person is not to be found anywhere. You yourself, as much as anybody in the entire universe deserve your love and affection." What stirs in you when you read this?

3. Right now, place your hand over your heart and offer self-compassion to yourself, saying "I am enough." Breathe in, breathe out. Allow a sense of "enoughness" to wash through you. Feel the transformative power of knowing you *are* good enough—just as you are.

Inner Listening

_____

_____

_____

_____

_____

_____

_____

_____

_____

_____

_____

_____

_____

_____

_____

Knowing

Self-compassion opens my heart to myself in a kind and loving way. It routs out feelings of selfishness, deservedness, and guilt. When I am tender with myself, I can be gentler with others.

DAY 15
Inner Progress

We're over halfway through our 30-day journey. This is a good time to pause, take some deep breaths and reflect on your inner progress.

So, how *is* your inner life these days? What kind of progress are you making each day to experience more peace of mind, or love or joy? To feel the presence of the Divine? The Persian poet Rumi reminds us that progress comes in steps and stages. He wrote: "A new moon teaches gradualness and deliberation, and how one gives birth to oneself. Patience with small details makes perfect a large work, like the universe."

This is true, especially when it comes to our inner growth. Patience is key and small changes, in time, become lasting changes.

What works well in terms of improving our inner life is doing a little less of one thing and a little more of something else. This way, the change we wish to make becomes not about getting it done right or quickly, but with Rumi-inspired gradualness. Most of us have spent far too many years pushing ourselves, having fallen prey to the pressures of perfectionism. Doing something gradually is, indeed, a self-compassionate act.

Going Deeper

1. As you assess your progress of the last 15 days, what can you tweak in your daily regimen? Perhaps a little less television watching and more reflection? Less time on the computer and more time in silence or connecting with nature? Transparently look at your daily activities to see if you are dedicating enough time to inner awareness and sacred connection.

2. At this halfway point, note any progress you are making. Are you feeling less stressed, more present? Less hard on yourself, more self-compassionate? Less focused on *doing*, more aware of *being*? Acknowledge these changes. Give yourself a big hug for the inner progress you've made!

3. Finally, how faithful have you been taking five minutes of Soul Time each day? It's never too late to begin again. Vary your daily schedule and find new ways to implement it if you can.

Inner Listening

_____

_____

_____

_____

_____

_____

_____

_____

_____

_____

_____

_____

_____

_____

_____

_____

_____

_____

Knowing

Inner progress takes time. It is important for me to be patient with myself, yet persistent in my practices. Vigilance and faithfulness are virtues of the spirit, as are gentleness and self-compassion. May I practice them all.

DAY 16
Light the Fire

When leading a workshop or retreat, I always begin by creating sacred space for us. I do so by lighting a Temenos candle. "Temenos" comes from a Greek word, which means "safe place" or "sanctuary." After lighting it, I recite these key words: "We light the fire of our soul life ... and enter our Temenos space ... to hear and tell our stories." This act creates a feeling of connection between us as participants and designates our time together as holy.

No matter the spiritual tradition, a lit flame universally represents the Divine. In mosques, temples, and churches around the world, you will find this burning flame. It serves to remind us that we are not alone and that we are in a place of sacred Presence, on holy ground.

Our homes can also serve as holy ground, sanctified as that by the lighting of a candle. Such a simple gesture, universally understood, invites us into deeper connection with our sacred self and Spirit right where we are. Each morning I greet the day by lighting a candle. I love that its warm glow fills the darkness of my home before dawn and makes the space I live in feel blessed. The same can be true for you. A simple act such as this can launch your day with purposefulness.

Going Deeper

1. Set the intention to begin your morning with a candle-lighting ritual to ignite the fire of your soul life.

2. Consider adding a prayer of greeting to your ritual, something like: "I am here, Divine One. Meet me where I am." Or a prayer of dedication: "I offer myself to You and the holy purpose of Love." Challenge yourself to create short morning prayers to begin your day in a meaningful way.

3. Reflect on your relationship with candles and light. How does it inform your relationship to the Divine?

Inner Listening

_____

_____

_____

_____

_____

_____

_____

_____

_____

_____

_____

_____

_____

_____

_____

_____

_____

_____

Knowing

I begin my day with the intention to recognize everything as sacred. I can honor this knowing by lighting a candle and establishing that where I sit or stand is holy ground.

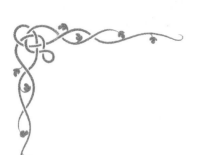

DAY 17
Divine Imagining

The human mind thinks in pictures. Most of us enjoy this scientific fact because the images we focus on can make us feel happier, more hopeful. The opposite is true as well. When it comes to a healthy inner life, having images to focus on can expand our understanding of the Divine—and who we are in relation to it. A stroll through any art museum will reveal how we humans have tried to portray the divine from the beginning of recorded time.

In Day 3, "Naming the Nameless," you explored your name for "God." Consider exploring your image of it too. What images do you currently hold of the Divine? Is it an image that fosters intimacy? Does it bring comfort and connection?

If it doesn't, set the intention to let a new one emerge. One that feels personal and meaningful. Your inner life is constantly evolving so your image of the Divine can too. The ultimate purpose of this journey is to get to know yourself as a spiritual being so you can live in alignment with that holy calling—to be a living, breathing embodiment of the One who lives and breathes through you. As Paramahansa Yogananda espoused, "Self-realization leads to God realization."

Going Deeper

1. Bring your attention to your heart center. Focus your awareness on how the Sacred is making itself known to you through an image right now. Breathe, and relax into that heart space by visualizing the Holy within you as clearly as you can. Would it be a "person"? A symbol? A color? An object?

2. Harness the powers of your imagination and let it flow freely. How does the presence of this image feel to you? What do your senses say about it? What body sensations arise when you focus on it?

3. The saints and sages of all traditions tell us that the surest "sign" of the presence of God is peace. Hopefully, the image of the Divine One that you hold will bring you that. If it doesn't, give yourself permission to expand your image. Ask for guidance. Invite inner wisdom to show you your way.

Inner Listening

Knowing

Holding an image of the Sacred within my heart helps me feel close to it. Though the Holy is mysterious, I can experience it on a human level as any of the virtues of the spirit—peace, love, or compassion—which, in turn, brings me to an ever-growing awareness of divine presence.

DAY 18
Nourish!

Thankfully, there is much conversation today in the media about how to live more healthfully: to eat right and exercise, to reduce our stress. But what about nourishing your inner life, feeding your individual soul?

Do you know what nourishes you? What easily restores your inner peace, your joy? And, if you do, do you actually do these things? Do you make time for them? Do you give yourself permission to nurture your inner being?

Many of us on a spiritual path know that we are here to serve. We are part of a grander purpose, and we often dedicate our lives to the care and "advancement" of others. In doing so, we tend to put ourselves, and our personal well-being, on the back burner, often to the point of depletion. How many nurses, social workers, teachers, counselors, caregivers, or pastors do you know who are overworked, stressed and unhealthy? Perhaps you are one of them.

Making time for spiritual nourishment is not a selfish thing, contrary to what we may have been taught. Spiritual nourishment is a self-aware thing—and it is very good to be self-aware! We cannot serve others well if we have not taken care of our *whole* selves—body, mind, heart, *and* soul. Without this, we may continue to give from a sense of depletion, even losing our health in the process.

Going Deeper

1. Do you give yourself permission to nourish yourself? Do you tend to neglect your own self-care? This is a common scenario in the helping professions or if you are a "born-nurturer."

2. Make a list of all the things/activities that nourish you—body, mind, heart, and soul. Examples: Quiet, solitude, reading, walking, napping, retreat time, spiritual conversation, nature, beauty, cooking, gardening, creativity, etc.

3. Which of these pleasures is speaking to you right now? In what does your heart long to engage? Listen to and honor that voice. Find ways to bring this form of nourishment into your life on a regular basis.

Inner Listening

_____

_____

_____

_____

_____

_____

_____

_____

_____

_____

_____

_____

_____

_____

_____

_____

Knowing

It is my divine birthright and destiny to be happy and whole. Regular spiritual nourishment calms and centers my body-mind and keeps my heart open, compassionate, and kind—to myself and toward others.

DAY 19
A Holy Invitation

It's true, human relationships are complicated. If we are dedicated to our growth, we know that in every human interaction, we will be invited to engage with others with our spiritual values intact. Every conversation with another invites us to be more than our personality or our history, more than our woundedness or our ego self.

With good self-observation and transparency, we'll get to see the light and the dark of ourselves. We can observe how we close our hearts to others, hold grudges, gossip, or slander. We also have the opportunity to open ourselves: to forgive, to be generous and loving.

Every difficult mind state we harbor holds a direct and holy invitation. With fear, love. With anger, peace. With control, acceptance. With judgment, open heartedness. With apathy, compassion. This is how we grow and become the people we are meant to be.

Going Deeper

1. The next time you're in conversation with someone and you feel the tug of ego, stop, take a breath, and accept the invitation of the emotion. Ask yourself, "Am I aligning with my ego (false self) by holding onto this emotion?" Listen for the voice of your wise self who invites you to embrace the correlating virtue instead.

2. The prayer of St. Francis is a prime example of how this process works. Reflect on how you can put the words of this prayer to use in your own life.

   "Where there is hatred, let me sow love;
   Where there is injury, pardon;
   Where there is discord, harmony;
   Where there is error, truth;
   Where there is doubt, faith;

Where there is despair, hope;
Where there is darkness, light;
And where there is sadness, joy."

3. Which strong emotion is offering you a holy invitation today?

Inner Listening

_____

_____

_____

_____

_____

_____

_____

_____

_____

_____

_____

_____

_____

_____

_____

_____

Knowing

In every human encounter I am being asked to ponder: "Am I living as my true self—whose essence is Spirit—and am I utilizing ALL the qualities of Spirit inherent within me? Or do I have "work" to do on myself?"

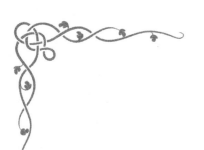

DAY 20
Sweet Release

There are many ways we can harness a breath practice to support us throughout the day. We learned one in Day 5. Today, consider using this one. I call it the "Ah, Breath." This is a more vocal way to breathe, not only to release tension, but to connect with the Holy One within. Think of the word, "Ah," and what it says to you. It speaks of relief and letting go. Say "Ahhhh..." and feel the tension in your face and shoulders release. Feel your belly soften. Feel the letting go that comes with this simple sound.

Now, think of another way you might say "Ahhhh." There is the "Ah" of pure delight and pleasure—tasting a forkful of delectable food or slowly sinking into a warm bath. This "Ahhhh" acknowledges the gift of physical and mental pleasures. It brings ease and relaxation, but it also allows gratitude to naturally arise.

When tension mounts in your body during the day, when your thoughts become frenetic, when your heart closes in disappointment, allow yourself the luxury of a long, vocal "Ahhhh..." Feel the relief that comes when you let go of what is troubling you. Let what constrains you roll out on wings of sound to be dispersed into the universe.

Going Deeper

1. Right now, and whenever you need it during the day, take a long, lengthy "Ahhhh" breath. Take three in a row for deeper relief. Be sure to vocalize the "Ah" with each exhale. Sit in silence afterwards and notice how you feel.

2. Experiment with the "Ah" breath. Give it more voice, more "umph," when you need to. Is the release greater? Follow it up with softer vocalizations of "Ahhhh." When you taper off the vocalization this way, do you feel more at ease? Meditative? Prayerful?

3. Anthropologists have found that many of the world's religions have names for the Divine that hold the "Ah" sound. God, Allah, Yahweh, Brahman, Avolokiteshvara, for example. There are thousands of cases of this, which may support the belief that the

"Ah" is a sacred sound—even the voice of pleasure as taken by the Creator in its creation.

Inner Listening

_____

_____

_____

_____

_____

_____

_____

_____

_____

_____

_____

_____

_____

_____

_____

Knowing

My breath has the power to restore and sustain me. Returning to a sacred breath practice throughout the day is not only good for what ails me but is a direct way to plug in to the God of my understanding.

DAY 21
Communing with Nature

Because human beings are creatures of Earth, the great outdoors is our natural home. Yet in the spirit of progress, we have increasingly cut ourselves off from nature. Many of us feel more "apart from" rather than "a part of" nature. We live and work indoors, away from a natural environment. This often brings feelings of disconnection from nature and Source.

In creation myths the world over, we often read of a creator god who shaped the world and took delight in its creations. We can too, by consciously reconnecting with nature and partaking of its beauty and restorative power.

On a physical level, studies demonstrate that spending time in nature creates a noticeable relaxation response. The body eases, the mind begins to rest, and a feeling of well-being washes over us. We can experience a noticeable heart opening too. The heart quivers in response to beauty. Awe and wonder naturally arise as a result.

On the highest level, we may feel the presence of the Creator. We are humbled by the work of divine intelligence, intimately connected to all of creation, grateful to be part of Indra's Web—united with all that is.

Going Deeper

1. Given the choice, choose an outdoor vs. an indoor activity. Like to read? Take your book outdoors. Like to nap? Lounge in a hammock. Need peace and quiet? Let birdsong, wind and waves calm your turbulent mind. Studies show that our relaxation response comes 50% faster if we take our activity outdoors.

2. Reflect on your relationship with creation. What effect does being in nature have upon you and your relationship with the Divine? Honestly assess if you spend enough time in nature for the purpose of sacred connection.

3. To enhance your time in nature, fine-tune each of your senses. Turn the volume of your senses to "high" to fully experience the sights, sounds and smells that nature offers you. As you find yourself enjoying and reconnecting with nature, give thanks for its beauty. Allow your spirit to soar as you witness its everyday miracles.

Inner Listening

_____

_____

_____

_____

_____

_____

_____

_____

_____

_____

_____

_____

_____

_____

_____

_____

_____

Knowing

Spending time in nature allows me to slow the pace of my life and be more aware of the joys found in the present moment. I can leave behind the stresses and strains of daily life and just BE.

DAY 22
Prayerfulness

There are many ways to pray and to meditate. Are prayer and meditation the same? A few years ago, I asked this question of one of my mentors, Sylvia Boorstein, a practicing Jew and Buddhist meditation teacher. She'd been using the words *prayer* and *meditation* interchangeably. I asked her about this. She said, "Whatever particular meditation practice we do, we are ardently hoping, indeed praying, for a peaceful and compassionate heart, for our own well-being and for the well-being of others. The very act of stopping to reorient ourselves—which is central to all meditation and prayer practices—and to focus our intention for the good, is a prayer."

Prayer or meditation, whichever term we use, is an act of reorienting ourselves. We turn our attention inward and drop into a space of remembering. What do we remember? We remember that we are divinely human, our beingness sourced in peace and love. We also remember that we are not alone on this journey. That we can connect with Source for guidance and comfort. We remember to trust our own good heart and recall how it, too, can guide us to act in ways that are wholesome and healing.

Prayer can be silent or vocal. Meditation can too. The Buddha taught that we can meditate any one of four ways: standing, sitting, walking or lying down. We can pray this way too. With conscious awareness, we can return to our sacred center anytime, anywhere.

Going Deeper

1. How would you describe your prayer life? Are you attentive to it? Do you make enough time for it? Transparently assess how prayerful you are.

2. We tend to forget how helpful prayer can be, especially when it comes to matters of discernment. What role does prayer have in your choice-making process? Dropping into inner quiet and allowing Spirit or our wise heart to guide us, is often overlooked.

3. If you could drop into prayer right now, what would your prayer be like? Spend the next few minutes in prayer/meditation and listen to your knowing heart.

Inner Listening

_____

_____

_____

_____

_____

_____

_____

_____

_____

_____

_____

_____

_____

_____

_____

_____

_____

Knowing

Prayer and meditation, engaged in regularly, help me stay in touch with my good wise heart, with my innate peace and love. I have the freedom to use whatever form lands me back in the lap of the Divine. Inner knowing and comfort are mine.

DAY 23
"What's Right?"

Gratitude as a spiritual practice can help us grow in faith and grace—no matter what is happening in our lives. You might wonder, how do you get to gratitude when life feels challenging? It's true, gratefulness can be difficult to grab onto when you're sick, behind on your bills, or worried about a loved one. You may find yourself focusing more often on what's wrong, rather than what's right, making life feel even more burdensome than it already is.

There was a time in our development as humans when we lived in caves and small communities, and physical harm was a reality. To ensure the continuation of the species, we needed to stay safe, so we were ever on the lookout for danger. Our human mind, though newly evolved, still relates to the world as a dangerous place. "What's wrong?" is our natural (default) inclination.

Because the mind operates this way, it tends to keep us focused on what's missing, not good enough, or potentially uncomfortable, which can lead to negativity, cynicism, or despair. To counterbalance this, we must learn to scout out "What's right." When we do, we'll find that we are able to create a new mindset—one that sees our world in a more positive light. A mind that inclines itself more and more to what is here, right now, so that we can appreciate our life as it is, without needing it to be different.

Going Deeper

1. With transparency notice how much you are able to look for the good, or if you have a tendency to focus on what's wrong in your life or in the world.

2. Retrain your brain to look for the good. Begin right where you are. Close your eyes. Take a few deep, calming breaths. Relax. Now open your eyes. Look around the room. Locate three things that are "right" or "good." These can be simple things like being able to read, being warm, having something nice to drink while you're sitting here. Close your eyes and repeat the practice. Reflect upon how doing this makes you feel.

3. You can do "What's Right" practice anytime, anywhere. Do it while waiting in line at the grocery story, when driving your car, or sitting in the doctor's office. Simply look around and point your heart toward what's good and life will begin to take on a brighter hue.

Inner Listening

_____

_____

_____

_____

_____

_____

_____

_____

_____

_____

_____

_____

_____

_____

_____

_____

_____

Knowing

My mental inclinations are mine to shift and retrain. I can focus on what's wrong or I can learn to see what's right in my world, thereby allowing a stream of gratitude to flow through my days.

DAY 24
Getting Still

"To the mind that is still, the whole universe surrenders," taught Lao Tzu. It's true, isn't it? When our mind is finally quiet, free of all the chatter, we feel deeply connected to All-That-Is. Many of us, however, have trouble getting quiet, which causes quite the conundrum because stillness is the cornerstone of a rich inner life.

As our day-to-day life picks up pace, our thoughts will too. The busier we get, the more thoughts we'll have to accommodate. The more experiences we have, the more input we allow in, the busier our minds will be. Stillness becomes harder and harder to access.

Without periods of stillness, we lose the ability to clearly hear the whispers of Spirit. Without inner calm, we lack the clarity we need to make wise discernments. Too much inner noise can block our perception and reception of grace.

How do you stabilize a busy mind? There is one sure-fire method to begin to access inner quiet: the practice of focusing. Focusing retrains the brain to settle down. With repeated effort, it inclines the mind toward behaving more like a calm sea than a raging river. Focusing can take us to the sacred shores of tranquility.

Going Deeper

1. Begin by focusing on one thing. Scan your immediate environment. Notice what your mind is naturally drawn to. (The mind responds positively to things that are appealing and feel good.) This could be a candle, a cookie, a photograph; a pattern of light playing upon the wall, a book on the shelf, a flower in a vase. Choose one to focus on intently. Notice everything about it. If your mind becomes bored and wants to wander off, gently guide it back to the object. If your thoughts become busy, simply bring them back to the practice. Do this for 2-4 minutes, strengthening your ability to "stay."

2. Practice focusing when you are out in the world. Do it in an airport, while sitting at a traffic light or waiting in line at the bank. The object of your focus doesn't matter.

Human or animal. Earth, tree, or sky. Focusing will retrain your brain. It will slowly introduce a greater sense of well-being into your life.

Inner Listening

_____

_____

_____

_____

_____

_____

_____

_____

_____

_____

_____

_____

_____

_____

_____

_____

Knowing

Paying attention on purpose retrains my mind to stay, to get still enough to hear the voice of the Divine. Focusing meditation helps me begin to see the world with sacred vision.

DAY 25
The Kindest Thing

I like to think of self-compassion as the missing ingredient in our lives—from healthcare to family care—we are simply not in touch with how being kinder toward ourselves helps. Many of us hold a hardened, "Just get over it, will you?" sort of attitude when it comes to how we handle personal difficulties. The truth is that everyone suffers. Everyone has a hard time now and then, including us.

How do you behave toward someone who is struggling? Would you talk tenderly to him or her, offer a hug? Make sure he or she feels supported and loved? But when it comes to yourself, what do you do? The practice of self-compassion invites us to open our hearts and embrace ourselves as we are, right in the midst of difficulty.

Self-compassion is a learned skill of extending tenderness in moments of suffering. It asks that we turn our own natural kindness toward ourselves. The voice of self-compassion speaks to us and says, "Remember, what you are experiencing *is* difficult. Stop, take a breath, and be tender with yourself."

Going Deeper

1. When you find yourself in a difficult situation, choose "the kindest thing." When you feel overwhelmed by life circumstance, stop, take a few calming breaths, and ask yourself this very important question: *"What is the kindest thing I can do for myself right now?"*

2. Listen carefully to the answer that emerges. If you are in tune with your spirit, it will guide you to something that is soothing. Perhaps you have to say "No" to others so you can say "Yes" to yourself. Or you need to step away, go into another room, lie down, take some time off. Take a walk, take yourself on a "date day," create an on-the-spot Sabbath. Even if it's as simple as going into the bathroom, locking the door, and sitting on the edge of the bathtub to breathe, do it.

3. Notice what is stirring in you about choosing the kindest thing. How does it feel to make a kind choice for self-care in the middle of difficulty? How does it feel to receive your own kindness?

Inner Listening

_____

_____

_____

_____

_____

_____

_____

_____

_____

_____

_____

_____

_____

_____

_____

_____

_____

Knowing

When I extend kindness toward myself, I open and soften. I become more hospitable, which, ultimately, allows me to be more hospitable and kinder toward others. Healing myself, I heal the world.

DAY 26
Opening and Letting Go

Sometimes our minds feel rigid and tight, too full of conversation, input, and chatter. As our technology-based society continues to pick up pace, offering us unlimited data and boundless opportunities to do more, life can begin to feel overwhelming. I call this feeling the "too-muchness of life."

When we feel that life is too much, we know that it would be good for us to turn inward—get still, pray, or meditate—but our mind and body are moving too quickly to do so. It is wise at times like these to give ourselves time and space to settle down. When the mind feels tight like a steel band, the body responding with tension, consider taking yourself to the edge, literally, to a place whose geography is spacious—vast, boundless, and open.

You can do this by placing yourself in the healing hands of Mother Nature. Stand on the top of a hill or mountain so you have a wide view. Go to the shore and stand at the ocean's edge. No mountain, no shore? Gaze at a rolling landscape. Focus on the horizon and locate the place where the sky meets the land. Turn your face to the sweeping blue sky. Allow the vastness of the universe to open you to feelings of interior spaciousness.

Going Deeper

1. When we are feeling shut down, it is up to us to open wide. Brain Gym experts tell us that every twenty minutes we should shift our focus from what we are concentrating on up close to that of a visual landscape. This reboots the brain, balances its functions, and brings the body-mind back into good working order.

2. To open: The Creator has placed within our glance the perfect tools for opening to inner peace through spaciousness: sky, mountains, shore and horizon. Place yourself in one of these and stand tall. Close your eyes. Open your arms wide, bend back a little, and open some more. Expand your heart center. Turn your face to the sky. Breathe.

3. To let go: Prayerfully invite the Divine One to enter your heart. Release what constrains or burdens you. Let it all go. Allow waves of release to wash over you. Give thanks for the bounty of nature, for the power of open spaces to restore and rejuvenate you.

Inner Listening

_____

_____

_____

_____

_____

_____

_____

_____

_____

_____

_____

_____

_____

_____

_____

_____

Knowing

It is good and wise to stop myself when I am feeling overwhelmed by life. The natural landscape of the earth is at my service, ever present, to soothe me, and help me return to feelings of spaciousness and ease.

DAY 27
A Breath Prayer

If you have read the work of Buddhist monk Thich Nhat Hanh, you know that the foundational practice he teaches for inner peace is accessing the breath. He encourages us to attach each inhale, each exhale, to words of healing. This way, our breath is not "empty," but laden with meaning. Our body-mind relaxes, releases its burdens, and comes back to center with each "breath statement."

Perhaps his most well-known "Gatha" (or sacred verse) is this:

"Breathing in, I calm my body.
Breathing out, I smile.

Breathing in, I dwell in the present moment.
Breathing out, I know it is a wonderful moment."

We can use a breath prayer like this to diminish strong emotions and move back into a place of equanimity. We can breathe in peace and breathe out our anger. We can breathe in love and breathe out disappointment. We can engage prayerfully with our breath, inviting the Divine One in to help us release what harms us, and begin to embody the qualities of spirit that will enliven us.

Going Deeper

1. Use Thich Nhat Hanh's breath prayer above. Pace your breath ever so gently and put words to each breath. Bring a slight smile to your lips as you say it. Notice how you feel.

2. Identify one strong emotion (mind-state) that you consistently struggle with. Create a breath prayer around it. For example: "I breathe in peace. I breathe out anxiety." Or "I breathe in ease. I breathe out fear." Visualize the positive mind state filling you up. Visualize the difficult emotion leaving your body. Feel the effects of that.

You can create a breath prayer like this for any mind state that threatens to keep you ego-bound and disconnected from your true essence.

Inner Listening

_____

_____

_____

_____

_____

_____

_____

_____

_____

_____

_____

_____

_____

_____

_____

_____

Knowing

My breath is sourced in the Divine. It is natural and wise to harness its power for my personal healing. A breath-based prayer practice is a gentle and useful way to release what ails me and to welcome in the good.

DAY 28
The Heart Knows

His Holiness the Dalai Lama, voted the most respected political *and* spiritual leader of our times, often speaks about how important it is to cultivate both rational wisdom and heart wisdom. Without a true blending of "mind" and heart, we have no real ability to navigate life skillfully. If we lack rationality, we might make foolish choices. Without inner knowing and compassion, we may harm ourselves, or others. In Eastern traditions, a blending of both is encouraged. Some have called this cultivating the "heart-mind."

How well do you know your heart-mind? In the West, we tend to focus on head over heart. We tend to dismiss the heart's wisdom, or, at the very least, consider it to be of secondary importance. Perhaps this is because we have not spent enough time tending to the landscape of our good, wise hearts.

In the words of Bhagawan Nityananda, "The heart is the hub of all sacred places. Go there and roam."

Going Deeper

1. Right now, connect with your good, wise heart. Do this by bringing your awareness to your head. Become cognizant of all the thinking that is going on in there. Now, bring your attention to your breath, specifically where it enters you at the base of your nostrils. Feel yourself breathing.

   Next, allow your awareness to move from head to heart, as if you were descending in an elevator, breath-by-breath, floor-by-floor. When you get to the bottom floor, the foundation of your being, your heart center, rest there.

2. Resting in your heart center, what do you notice? A feeling of inner peace? Of gratitude? A sense of homecoming?

3. Ask your heart, "What would you like me to know right now?" Wait. Listen for its wise response. Reflect on the answer that comes.

Inner Listening

_____

_____

_____

_____

_____

_____

_____

_____

_____

_____

_____

_____

_____

_____

_____

Knowing

Knowing how to listen to and accept my heart's wisdom is a valuable commodity.
When I spend so much time in my thinking brain, the essence of my heart can become
unknown to me. My heart-mind holds the perfect blend of human knowledge and divine
wisdom.

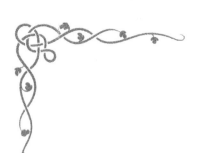

DAY 29
Patiently Waiting

If we are honest with ourselves, most of us do not like to wait, though we are given ample opportunity to practice patience all day long. In line at the grocery store, in traffic jams, in doctors' offices, we become immediately restless and agitated when things are not progressing the way we think they should.

The same can be true when it comes to our inner lives. We grow impatient to see progress. When it comes to discernment, we want immediate answers. We want to get rid of pain in a hurry and get to joy just as quickly. Ironically, something we are not very good at—being patient—is esteemed as one of the "highest" spiritual virtues.

Patience is precisely what is required of us if we are to stay faithful to our spiritual path. We must learn to stay, to wait, for the divine timing of our own unfolding. Things happen that we don't plan on. Detours are taken. Timelines and goals are not always met. We are certain we are ready for the relationship, the career, or the cure, yet "life" intervenes to whisper, "Not now." So, we wait, either with patience and trust, or resistance and frustration. The choice is ours.

Going Deeper

1. How are you at waiting, especially when it comes to your spiritual life? Do you trust in the timing of your own unfolding? Reflect on this.

2. Who is holding the steering wheel of your spiritual life? Is it primarily you in control? Do you let Spirit lead and take charge? Assess your current ability to let go and let God.

3. Practice waiting. Wherever you find yourself, notice any irritability that arises. Return to the "effortless practice" of breathing for stabilization. Use the "Ah, Breath" to release frustration. Come back to "the now" of your present experience and simply feel grateful for the gift of be-ing.

Inner Listening

_____

_____

_____

_____

_____

_____

_____

_____

_____

_____

_____

_____

_____

_____

_____

_____

_____

_____

Knowing

Patience is a spiritual practice that is beneficial to cultivate so I can feel more at ease in my life. I grow through every human experience, especially those I don't like or plan for. There is divine order woven into the fabric of my days.

DAY 30
This Precious Moment

It is difficult for most of us to live in the present moment. Granted, our physical bodies are in the here and now, but our minds are elsewhere. We are either dwelling on the past or thinking about the future. The 60,000 thoughts we think each day are primarily focused on what we could have done, just did, or will be doing. We are rarely fully present, truly aware of this very moment.

Each moment is precious, but do we regard it as such? We logically know that our life will have a finite number of days on this earth. We know that we may not even be here tomorrow. Life is unpredictable and ever-changing. But we do not treat it as such—a limited commodity, a sacred container of moments—that will never exist again.

Ironically, the present moment is the only place where we can experience the presence of God. If we are distracted, we miss the cues that say divine companionship is right here, right now. We forget that timeless wisdom is accessible through our sacred breath. We lose sight of our true nature, our calling, and our path, when the needle of our inner compass points to regret, shame, fear or worry—powerful indicators that we are not fully present in the marvelous Now. And the Now is the only place where the Living Spirit resides.

Going Deeper

1. Are you aware of how your own preoccupation with the past or the future can keep you disconnected from Spirit? How does this play out in both your inner life and your outer life?

2. Learn to bring your awareness back to the present moment. Stop yourself at any given moment and assess where your attention is placed. Are you reworking yesterday's conversations or fretting over tomorrow's activities? Refocus. Bring your attention back to this very moment. Say to yourself, "Be here now," and feel the ease and blessing of that.

3. Bringing greater mindfulness to your daily tasks is a good way to stay more present. Washing dishes? Consciously feel the warm, soapy water moving between your fingers. Mowing the lawn? Smell the sweet fragrance of grass clippings. Heighten your senses to appreciate the activity you are engaged in. Feel the presence of the Sacred in all of it.

Inner Listening

_____

_____

_____

_____

_____

_____

_____

_____

_____

_____

_____

_____

_____

_____

_____

Knowing

Living in the present takes practice. Each moment is unique and special, never to be repeated. The past cannot hold me. The future need not concern me. I am at "home" whenever I allow myself to be fully present.

Afterwards...

Our 30-day journey has come to an end. I'd like to invite you to take some time to integrate and reflect upon your "time in." My hope is that your inner life has deepened in significant ways—that your relationship with yourself as a sacred being has expanded, and that your relationship with the Divine has grown as well.

With transparency and self-compassion, assess how you did connecting with "your deepest you" this month. It is good and wise to acknowledge your inner growth and celebrate your victories. It is also good and wise to acknowledge your ongoing areas of struggle. Vow to transform these until ease of body, mind, heart, and spirit are yours.

Feel free to use the blank pages in the back of the book to reflect on these questions:

1. How do you feel about yourself having completed this 30-day inner journey?

2. How are you experiencing the Divine today because of this journey?

3. In which areas of your inner life did you experience growth? Positive change?

4. In which areas of your inner life are you still having difficulty?

   Or feeling resistance?

5. Describe what you learned about the role of spiritual practice in your life.

6. Where and how did you experience grace or blessings this past month?

7. What is one of your "growing edges?"

8. What commitment to your inner life are you willing to make as you go forward?

ADDITIONAL JOURNALING PAGES

*We must be willing to get rid of the life we've planned,
so as to have the life that is waiting for us.
The old skin has to be shed before the new one can come.*

— Joseph Campbell —

What might you need to shed to experience holy newness?

What is the condition of the temple of your heart?

The analogy of the building of an interior temple,
a temple of the heart, as a house for the Divine is
a useful description of the work involved in creating
the inner life, a living spiritual life.

— Regina Sara Ryan —

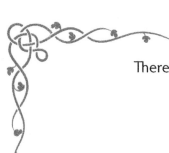

There are never enough names and images for what we love.

— Dorothee Soelle —

By what names would the Sacred call you?

What might you need to turn away from so your soul is strengthened?

Run my dear,
From anything
That may not strengthen
Your precious budding wings.

— Hafiz —

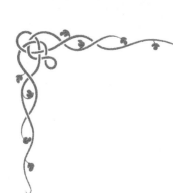

Divinity is my true nature. I am a soul among souls.

— Julia Cameron —

Who do you know yourself to be?

Have you been paying attention to the whisperings of your heart-mind?

What does it have to say to you today?

Shifting our identification from the ego to the heart-mind
is the beginning of individual spiritual work.

— Ram Dass —

Spiritual practice is the heart of spiritual life.
Spiritual practice is to the mystical life what
food and water are to the body. These are the inner source
of nourishment and growth.

— Brother Wayne Teasdale —

How is your spiritual practice like food or water to your soul?

How faithful are you being to your inner growth?

True devotion and commitment are never made with the mind.
These qualities, which allow us to expand, to grow,
and to bloom into our potential, are developed
through the heart and the spirit.

— Jamie Sams —

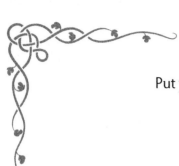

Put your ear down close to your soul and listen hard.

— Anne Sexton —

What does your soul have to say to you today?

How could you bring more "Light" into your days?

Do not fight the dark. Just turn on the light.

Let go, and breathe into the goodness
that you are.

— Swami Kripalvananda —

All shall be well. And all shall be well. And all manner of things shall be well.

— Julian of Norwich —

What breath prayer would serve you well right now?

What role does gratitude play in your spiritual life?

Gratitude bestows reverence,
allowing us to encounter everyday epiphanies,
those transcendent moments of awe that change forever
how we experience life and the world.

— John Milton —

If we are to persevere for the long haul, we must not overdrive our souls.

— Joan Chittister, OSB —

How do you feel when you offer yourself compassion?

What is opened in you?

What steps are you taking to bring yourself into alignment with the Divine?

Each glimpse allows us a step further on the bridge
uniting us with this eternal goodness.

— Joyce Rupp, OSM —

About the Author

Since 1994, Janice Lynne Lundy, DMin, MPC, has been helping people around the globe transform their inner lives, gently guiding them to deepen their relationship with the Divine as they understand it. She does this professionally as a spiritual director, pastoral counselor, educator, and retreat leader with an interfaith-interspiritual focus.

Passionate about the written word, Jan is the author of nine spiritual growth books, including *Your Truest Self: Embracing the Woman You Are Meant to Be*. She has been described as "practical and poetic, possessing deep and gentle wisdom." Each of her books supports our universal journey to live with calm, clear minds, and wise, compassionate hearts.

Jan is the co-founder and co-director of The Spiritual Guidance Training Institute which offers education and certification in interfaith-interspiritual direction (guidance). She is also Visiting Professor of Spiritual Direction at The Graduate Theological Foundation.

Jan resides in northern Michigan, delighting in the quiet beauty of the region and rejoicing in her ever-growing family.

Learn more about the author at her website: www.JanLundy.com

Made in the USA
Coppell, TX
12 March 2023

14176872R00050